To Rosemary

Promised Dream

Joseph J.
Capriccio

Promised Dream

Joseph J. Capriccioso

To order additional copies of this book, contact:
Xlibris Corporation
1-888-795-4274
www.Xlibris.com
Orders@Xlibris.com
118386

Table of Contents

Come out of the rain to the brightest sun. Here your wars are already won. Nothing exists but just you and the new. How will this joy shape you?

A new series is born from a sorrow storm. You are transformed! With happiness restored you're floored! Have you finally scored?

The Tomorrow's Song Series

There is a new beginning for the man of nothing as he meets the girl of tomorrow.

Fresh to battle evil's effect, the energy is limitless. With ease and rest, she blocks his wreck. The shadow can't damage the fully healed. Holy weapon of golden times invites no terror or evil to the ascension of second chances. Ride the wave of happiness, for it is long overdue. A positive future you hear in song, never give up and be strong. After your horrible extremes, you can still reach a promised dream.

About Promised Dream

Nearing the end of *9 Years Time* of depression, I published *Sorrow of Separation* and was working on *Tomorrow's Song*. My life had dramatically changed with my first book's release. When I wasn't looking for love, it hit me. After so many years of sadness, happiness flowed at a rapid rate. Even though the relationship was brief, it did teach me that there are better things on my horizon. I changed the book to be the opposite of sorrow as this was what would come tomorrow. The series did split with the release of this. While some books were like sorrow, others were positive like tomorrow. *Destiny's Calling* is the sequel to *Tomorrow's Song*. *Greatness and Glory* was the sequel to *Destiny's Calling*. Having the books out of order made the series a lot more interesting. Still, I always felt I wanted to do more with *Tomorrow's Song*. It was nearing the release of *9 Years Time* that inspiration hit, and I decided to revisit *that great exciting new chapter of my life being in love with this girl of tomorrow*. Promised Dream is enjoying life in a positive atmosphere feeling young and adventurious. The Man of Nothing becomes something as he has a fresh start. He changes his second book Tomorrow's Song based on his happiness that flows freely. The shadow can't find him to hex but he won't give up . . . yet.

I hope you will enjoy Tomorrow's Song 2:Promised Dream and look for Book 3 Coming Soon!

Acknowledgments

I would like to give special thanks to my friend Liz for showing me how much better my life can be.

Please check out all the nine books of the Sorrow of Separation series.

They are the following:

- *Sorrow of Separation* (May 5, 2010)

- *Tomorrow's Song* (October 21, 2010)

- *Winds of Change* (January 29, 2011)

- *Destiny's Calling* (April 29, 2011)

- *Loss of Ways* (July 13, 2011)

- *Shadow's Reign* (February 17, 2012)

- *Greatness and Glory* (April 17, 2012)

- *Dark Days* (May 9, 2012)

- *9 Years Time* (Sept 10, 2012)

Unexpected

For every day that life will stray with sadness that is all-consuming, there is one particular day that love is blooming. Darkness tried to keep it hidden, but love knows no intermission. The sun lights a life, warming it to flight. Take arms, for victory sings you out of losing. Now and forever you are choosing. Pride is alive as you thrive to dive into the wonder. The wary man walks again for one more round. This is the last chance. Wear your best vest, for the unknown may take action against your attempt. You crave a life deserved. Winds can blow, but still you go. Rain can drench, but you survive the trench. A storm tried to drown you, but God found you. A holy light enveloped your life, halting a car's disaster from shadow's massacre. Continue strong despite what goes on. Wave it off, for you're no longer soft. Tougher than any other, you are a father. You will not give up on the ones you love so much. Many will try to stop you, but they will all fail. A father's love will prevail. For now enjoy time unexpected as a tomorrow girl can fine-tune a heart dissected. A kiss to return what was missed.

A wanting and craving to a happiness waiting. Now it all speeds back to leave you sidetracked. What the hell was that? You grab her back for another. Now the feeling is shared. There is more to this embrace. No minutes measured as you stare into each other's eyes. You died before, but now can you come alive? You survived and existed, building to this one moment. This one second that you could love again and a past can be forgotten. A heart can mend and beat again. This girl has made an impression. Were you to come out of your pit to be welcomed by this? The girl of your dreams. Is it possible that you are worthy of her attention? To feel wanted and needed by just being you. She pursued you, and you didn't think it would go anywhere, but you gave it a try. Wow, how she opened your eyes to worlds away that you could be part of today. You must return home, but you embrace a few more times. As you ride the bus, you sigh. To think when you least expected it, love heals all wounds and your life changes its tune.

She is on your mind the seconds you're separated. Is this your one true chance for that dance? You smile on your way home as the future is unknown. Just then you fall out of view of the evil tracking you. No sadness, no despair, just care. With ease, you breathe. Can you finally overcome being the lonely one?

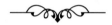

Quiet Reflections

There were days I thought I lost you forever. My life wouldn't have mattered. Without you two, I could not continue. My sole reason to stand against the unstoppable was your love to make it possible. With your faith in me, I could overcome any adversary. God had stepped in, and I continue on battling the sin. This smile knows the outcome. It is glorious, for victory will be mine. I will dress for effect. My will can protect against their wreck. I was knocked down round after round, but still I kept laughing, for the moment I get up, they would no longer be tough. My mind is always made up of easing the rough. Many don't play fair, and I challenge their dare. This man won't go away, for he has nothing. No title, no respect, but still he'll interject. He says no to evil's plague, for he will cure darkness impure.

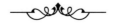

Just a Little Push

Never forget sorrow's game for the principal thing is to keep surviving. Always brave life's haze, for clarity doesn't always come. Special moments exist to spring board your life out of line. Hear the song that you belong and melody your life to reasoning. Life is a symphony, and some strings are out of tune. Continue on through discrepancy of happiness, for you will reach the forgotten string to everything. Once life flows complete, no one can knock you to the street. Love will fill the void. Passion consumes your air, and of all your problems, you don't care. What matters is the woman in your arms as your shield is disarmed. To open up your heart again, you pray you will win. Feelings grow serious, for you wished for this. A fire returns but not to burn. Warm is the embrace, speeding the pace. Time stands still as this is your reward. The enemy doesn't know your address as you're free from hex.

Out of Thin Air

Not looking for the sunrise and then surprise. The reversal from negative effects washed away to ignite the life denied me. Out of the blue, when chances are few, comes happiness unexpected. During this time, the darkness ceased to be, as if blocked from my positive sea. Nothing could prevent this event. Did the evil even try? No trace of waste or vibes from the chilling knives of hater's stabbing. A calm after the storm as joy constructed adventures romantic. The delicious of lips and absence of air. Embraced abruptly into your forgotten dreams. A tease as you are sent away. Dumbfounded, you would return without question. If your planner was full, you'd throw out the book. Intrigue will lead to a hook. You will bite and eat the pole. To savor the happiness temporary, each second will be remembered.

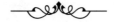

Thank You

I wasn't looking for this, but you sent her my way.

So much time falling, yet this time I was soaring.

The up from my down, the biggest turnaround.

Missing was the evil and negative hex that sent my life downward.

Feelings overwhelmed to relaxed as life was absent of suffering.

My life reached its high, and reality warped to court my happiness.

Everyone enjoys their time in the sun.

More powerful than ever, have I won?

For the first time I lived in the moment as the present was much more intriguing.

The vision was clear, not needing a lens to steer.

Adventures took me beyond my map as destiny showed worlds away.

City of lights, no limits to where I could grow.

I had everything I finally wished.

Now I would work even harder to safeguard my existence.

Creations were born to calculate the storm and predict its return.

For now I took it all in enjoying my win.

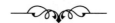

Code of Clarity

Honor thy name, for you will always wear it.

Keep your confidence, for if you believe, you can achieve.

Have faith, for prayer can change the unchangeable.

Never measure your limits, for willpower can't be recorded.

There is no such word as *can't*.

Stop to see the nonsense and laugh as you take away its chaos.

If you fall, never linger.

Don't be chained to a schedule, for life is unexpected.

Help as many as you can but not the enemies looking to destroy you.

Open your mind to all outcomes and be aware of the impossible.

The only surprise in life is your failure to not detect it.

Carry no weapons but sharpen your words carefully.

If you can build from the dirt, your life will have worth.

Ride of Your Life

Soar to a life dreamed of before.

Fast is the pace, for there is no time for darkness.

Evil won't find you.

Sorrow is missing from your emotional plate.

You just ate from the freshness of peace, for happiness is sweet.

The nectar of forever filled with love unmeasured.

You're a world away from the sadness of yesterday.

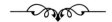

Happiness Doesn't End

The sun of a new day with the freshness of purpose.

A restart from a race leading in circles.

I break away to curve into what's denied me.

A relationship is born of paradox's placement.

Energy is on overflow as I go into the light.

Nights are bright, no more alone pondering.

I don't have time to think of history's joke.

My future I can see more clear and free of hater's curse.

This girl that pursued me could be my destiny.

In the moment is where I live while senses overload with what should be.

Of this message I can hear as a writer now and forever I be.

Open Your Window

Listen, can you hear your feelings clear?

Emotions building for what's missing.

A love all new yet familiar to you.

Just let the love in and experience your win.

Don't hold back and let happiness rush in.

Lower your shields, for the darkness is gone.

Consume this joy too soon and mesmerize lost in her eyes.

How could anyone be so wonderful and have feelings for you?

Her looks are spectacular, so this is what comes after?

Walk to her and put effort into evolving.

Let this book take shape of the love made to wait.

Your tomorrow is today, oh how you wish it'll stay.

More days like this, living in bliss.

Still, you have to wonder where the darkness goes as it is absent from this flow.

This blessing only God knows.

You were destined to meet—that much is certain.

You won't question.

For just once, you won't question.

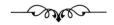

Pillow Thoughts

Late at night you're well rested.

Evil was bested and ceases to be.

This is your heaven on earth.

Lying next to your best.

You met your match and sleep sound.

This life is rebuilt from the ground.

Nightmares cease, for finally you know peace.

Flowers in bloom with a constant tune.

The song that will carry me higher than I dreamed.

With my weight lifted, my mind soars to a future explored.

No more alone, with sadness a distant memory.

Rise and Define

Morning walk with the cooling air.

The smell of her hair that gives you a high.

You survived.

Now you will thrive and take it all in.

You win.

Happiness is all you know.

Nothing else matters, but that doesn't stop the chatter.

A call again from my purple-haired friend.

I hope this good luck is a trend.

The mind has no history to focus on.

No backward as forward is where I walk.

Blocked is the hardship to curse you.

Responsibility takes a vacation as for once you have time.

Moments to smell, food to savor with a love's savior.

Is it possible, after all you've been through, your life is sublime?

Still with a watchful eye, you wait for a storm that doesn't come.

Is evil on a vacation too?

Can this world expand to be forever lasting?

Look at her smile that gives you confidence.

You feel like you can leap high from the ground and land on two feet.

A world you explored once before where a future you could settle in.

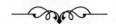

Tomorrow Girl Defined

She is the pleasant to my plain ordinary.

The drink that quenches my adventure.

An excitement I wasn't expecting, changing my canvas. The probability not predicted.

With my shields I resisted, but she kept at me. She worn down my defenses, and I would meet my tomorrow girl today. On an ordinary street, I stood on two feet, walking into my unknown. A chant in the air made it seem like a theme leading me to winning. I wasn't looking for this and was ready to be let down. Never did I expect her to become a girlfriend yet. Breakfast would fill our curiosity. This date was extended. Not a typical day I expected to go my way.

Darkness Puzzled

Shadow: Resist my mist?

Hide from plain sight?

My ways are blocked from seeping in objection.

You are shielded from darkness and . . . rain?

Who is this girl that powers your protection from dark intervention?

To come through your dreams and prevent my nightmares?

Someone else has power and is playing a deadly game.

The light blesses love to your name.

You have no doubt or fear.

The answer is Crystal clear.

The Heart Healed

You chase me from afar while thoughts were on my loss.

The crazy reality that opportunity comes while I'm not searching.

All my requests answered the moment we kiss.

Suspended from decline, I absorb love unexpected.

I breathe as if for the first time.

So warm is snuggle from the woman who embraces me.

Each second cherished into memory the heaven that escaped me.

I'm healed and young, enjoying the fun.

You make my masterpiece.

The anthem that jettisons my destruction.

There is no world alone.

My cup is filled.

Finally I survive the victor.

Tears flow of this happiness I now know.

Thank you for this day and more to come.

I gaze at the stars and no longer wish.

Life accepts this gift.

My sleep is sound.

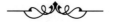

A music box soothing.

The melody of peace that I will be okay.

No matter what will come, I will never be done.

I will forever love what you have done to me and how you shape me.

Even if we never last, I can live past any challenge thrown.

I'm younger yet fully grown.

Past to Present

Somewhere in time was a man so sad.

Tomorrow he will survive through the bad.

Marching on that long road, he struts gold.

Burning bright is the light that makes him bold.

Smile, for you must always be the man that fights reality.

Never stop moving through storms, for you're born to thrive.

Realize that this world is forced to accept you.

You would never give up on those kids you love so much.

This title of father you hold so high.

Forever battling her evil lies.

Past or future, you won't be a loser.

Know what must be done for sons and do it.

Enjoy this time with the new but prepare for the darkness that will return for you.

Christmas in July

Spellbound by this turnaround, no end is expected quick.

You've wanted for so long to hear this song.

Rules fly out of view, for a ruler is you.

The king of your own thing.

In total control after climbing out of hole.

You light up my might to achieve.

This girl is all I need.

All I must do is to be with you.

Can this lead to white doves and blue skies?

A suit so sharp next to a gown so alive.

Open Window / Clear Sky

Not knowing time, just the rubbing of lips.

Moisture and the power of touch very much loved.

Exploring each strand of your hair, you drool like a fool.

On the couch, there is only the breeze and holding of this gorgeous unfolding.

There is no past, present, or future, just time at a standstill.

You don't even know your name, just instinct of pleasure.

Love revisits the emotional home.

You want it to stay and make a play for future's outcome.

She is what you desire.

Awakened is the bachelor not grounded or tied to settling down.

Hot and heavy progresses the nourishment of passion.

If there is an audience, enjoy the show.

The clothes will flow, but this couple will warm to steam extreme.

A sleepover with many different meanings.

For the first time in a long time, satisfaction comes regularly, and you forget past's hang-up.

You are dancing without movement.

To sing without uttering a word.

All temperatures hot and cold are married to comfort.

To make an announcement that finally challenge accepted for your rested.

Make a note that you're connected and love is building to a possibility.

Wanting Happiness

All that I want to do is be in love with you.

As far as I can see, you are with me.

My universe has order, for the fun has begun.

You dropped in and changed everything.

To fill up my mind with a woman of a different kind.

Magic has to be, for I am drawn to thee.

I don't need to look, for I have found my turnaround.

The volume is loud but healing.

Words fit that I missed.

Puzzles are solved with ease.

A clear heading to my Avalon.

For once I won't walk alone.

The daze that I'm lost in succeeding.

A new relationship holds meaning.

Quiet Stroll

I will walk and talk ascending into laughter.

Will this finally be happily ever after?

To try not to rush this journey, I sit comfortably.

Even a simple walk with her has me gleaming.

All the enemies are gone that annoy me?

Very strange to feel a shield blocking suffering.

Each day in conversation is education.

I learn more and more of this girl I adore.

There is some concern as I'm wanting what I already have.

To miss her if I don't see her?

That feeling is all too familiar as I won't resist her.

Love hits me square in the face, and I welcome it.

To put my armor away and dress light may destroy me one night.

I decide to give this feeling a chance.

Can it lead to a dance?

Sorrow of Separation 11: Edge of Reason

The future hidden from view as life fell around you. Disgusted, tired of rebuilding, you stood boiling. Shaking in rage from the madness of hatred built up from the darkness that sought to destroy you. You took the mask, so very exhausted with losing. The eyes closed as you laid down placing to mask down. All the emotions held back to strike, all the feelings of white faded from sight. Tears and then a smile.

Laughter that echoed the anger. Born is the oncoming storm. No trace of nice or sentiment. Somewhere the world will shake as angel and shadow alike won't accept this night. A dream, nightmare, or reality shaped of hate?

Future Is Saved

There is a feeling that the evil will go away.

You will celebrate the victory over all the battles you fought.

You don't know how this will come to be.

For now, enjoy these times in the sun, for evil is not yet done.

Darkness can't accept your win yet.

On this day the sun is so bright.

Another will come with your greatest fight.

Just hold her hand to cherish these moments you can't resist.

A hater is being groomed, so you meet your maker.

Double and triple teams will hit in a future stream.

Now is only your paradise of life.

Problems don't exist of any manner.

Too perfect to be believed, yet it's as real as the trees.

Joyous Segment in Time

When you think you can't blink.

If the pain comes crashing in, remember this moment of satisfaction to give you traction.

A memory that must be born again.

Happiness to be loved and a world that turns at your pace.

All the great times start flooding in as every day your song is loud.

Motivated to continue a saga written of your worst disasters.

Heart and soul carved in time to remind.

Will this love extend to a happy end?

This drive you have of alive has never been so focused.

As if the good luck was held back, it hits in every way imagined.

Shielded from any headache or hang-up, you finally stand straight.

Not a cloud in the sky and you don't wonder why.

Preview of the Promised Wonder

To enemies born and haters new, I have a present for you.

I won't go away, and my decision is etched in stone.

This is what I wish to do, to write a series to help you.

Through the sadness of doubt, you can shout out.

I will fight with all that's holy to bombard the darkness totally.

Hear my voice and see your choices.

There is always another way.

Close your eyes and pray to be blessed to say . . .

I believe in the Lord and shall survive my discord.

No enemy will end me or cause me to quit.

I'll never give up on this life lit.

Love will remain despite the pain.

My day will come out of the sorrow's past.

There is always a light that can burn fast out of darkness cast. Words won't hurt me to fail, for my future of success I hail.

The road will be hard, but I'm on guard.

For my kids I will win it all and keep going.

Curses and hexes won't have an effect, for I am watched by an angel from above.

I will fall in love with a true that was long overdue.

Crystal's Sunrise

My father that suffered so much, look up.

Feel me protect thee, for you deserve so much more.

Live this life denied and realize you must always strive to be on top.

Enemies may grow, but just know you will succeed.

Love is all you . . . need?

What's this I see of a future clouded in mystery?

A divergence of stream leading to a strange society.

The rage unrecognized released from hatred's pain to alter your frame.

This I didn't foresee, for a happy life must be.

Magic erratic and unnatural creates this storm.

My greatest nightmare so unfair, you must never wear.

Love returns when you least expect it.

A relationship can improve your very existence.

So much can be accomplished as if life flows to your stream.

Everything connects to no longer reject.

You're welcomed into a peace you never thought you'd meet.

No more are you falling as you hear a calling.

Your purpose and destiny shouting for you to hear.

A future so crystal clear that there is no doubt what you must do.

Find you and what you like to do.

Give it your best shot and be open to everything.

Open the Blinds

This future I can finally make out.

I will shape my direction to ascension.

Still I will never forget the man that wanted me free.

Free of negativity and problems that arise.

You protected me as best as you can, Dad.

I will not wither away as I'm here to stay.

My fight will be very hard, but the reward will be glorious.

The last laugh of hardship's past for my future will flourish.

Step into the New

Beyond the routine of familiar path to travel down a road never glanced at.

To the noise and brightest of lights escaping the silence of lonely nights.

Strange buildings taller than imagined while life is so busy.

Another world I never explored as I'm floored at this life that passed me by.

Out of my element, I adapt to this.

Everyone matters as this city excites me.

Styles are strange while others are tame.

I will brave and expand my journey grand.

If a thought can give life to this, then reality is filled with dreams.

Learn that you can always grow no matter what you know.

The world will always surprise me.

Luck or Skill

Was it luck or skill that created my first thrill?

Can I recreate the magic beyond new for book 2?

Inspiration pushes pen to write a fourth trend.

Is this what my destiny is?

If I could write of sorrow and tomorrow, will the world change?

Will a book help you back from your darkest setbacks?

Can I lead you into the light you can't see?

I just have to try and not question why.

My end never came as God stopped the insane from killing me completely.

Another chance that I never wasted for life becomes elevated.

I did rise from my pit to create this.

My *Sorrow of Separation* will make preparations out of depression.

There is more in life that you're in for.

Be stronger to last longer, for the greatest threat hasn't come yet.

Build your weakness into strength for the skills you'll need to succeed.

There will be roads rougher, villains tougher, with haters that hunger for your throat.

Have the power of wise to conquer your cries and stand triumphant.

Feel good and burn your dreams into reality's fabric.

Long for the confidence to defeat the hysterics of chaos unfolding.

Undiscovered Paradise

I never knew of this life so cool.

Lying with my wonderful in a comfy comforter.

Stars are bright yellow as I don't need to wish thanks.

I got what I wanted, and it took awhile.

My smile never extended this much.

I don't complain, for there is no rain.

Understand that this I didn't plan.

To live after I survived a happy man.

Affection feels good as I moved on.

So long it took to belong.

My life was cracked like broken glass, but she had the glue.

She got me when many didn't understand me.

I'm still so tense as if still on defense.

I look but can't see any darkness looking for me.

My guess is you can't infect this address, for you can't find it.

Is she all that I'm looking for?

What if she wants more?

Will she explore a world without my core?

This is pleasant, and I shouldn't ruin this slow motion of happiness.

Is she the right of all my wrongs?

Can I truly belong?

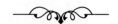

A Shadow Restless

Far away the evil will sway for its chance to alter.

A shadow so cunning that he will destroy a man to nothing but still not be able to kill him.

No matter what is thrown, even if there is nothing to own, this man will bounce back.

He will get up and never have enough, for the goal will always be in reach.

His soul will teach that you must have spirit and drive to survive.

Just realize your happiness may be a world away, but forget the distance and go.

Blessed to protect his sons born, he will brave any storm.

He hears his calling but still doesn't know what to do.

Sometimes you need to go through a few breaks to see the true stakes.

Heal up, go back to plan.

After every challenge you still stand.

Love This Life

My life had its ups and downs, but this flower had rooted me from the sea.

I was on my road back and then contact from this stranger to be my savior.

Teaching me the finer things not noticed.

Sometimes you need to put down the glasses to see the bigger picture.

Chemistry needs the right mixture for bliss.

We often wander in search of our path.

Confused, we travel looking for that clue.

In this case she found you.

You can't search for love, for love finds you.

Passion can rebuild you.

Confidence will skyline to tower over adversity.

No matter where you go or how much you grow, you still have to face what made your life erase.

This Pathway I Chose

One day it will all make sense why you took this journey.

Peace and tranquility as sorrow still hasn't followed me.

I could learn to make a life from this height.

A sound sleep with no losing streak.

Will I wake up to learn this is just a dream?

Here comes the rain.

Nope, this is real.

Her umbrella is the biggest I have ever seen.

A calm before the storm as the world looks to get dark.

The trees blow as the leaves fly to color my sky.

Winds of change have always found me and turned my life upside down.

She sees me distressed and grabs my hand to warm my land.

The clouds go away to a sunny day?

Do I have faith that she is meant for me?

I have no fear when she is near, for I want to make her world better.

No matter the weather or cloud covers, I will still hover with you by my side.

I'm alive and I will remain happy with you.

This joy is long overdue.

Let no one try to maim this wonderful life sane.

What is to be I can't see, but for once I live in the present.

This girl gives me a purpose to shine past my nine.

Years of depression and now jubilation.

My life is more than I ever thought before.

So much more I could write.

I could get used to this life.

To settle in and write a series where I've been.

My past, present, and future out of order like one big puzzle to figure out.

To let it flow freely, for I will have no doubt.

Future's March

If I could prepare you for life, would I tell you of struggle?

Times that exist that you just don't have all the answers?

To live with a sorrow that you don't think will ever pass?

No, I will tell you what you are born for.

You are destined to live and reach the highest star.

No matter the pain or persecution, you must know that failure is the illusion.

Your family crest have battled the best and conquered evil's armies.

We have always won because we believe in the one.

One God that created all.

One God that will lift us after our greatest fall.

One made of pure love and light.

A love that survives even in the darkest night.

Our Lord makes time for each and everyone.

I have pledged to make this world better.

My weapon is my voice, for I will give them a choice as he gave me.

Face the darkness, for you are stronger.

You will fall no longer.

The odds don't mean a world of spit.

Keep going even if you had it.

Never let up and continue to shine.

To ignore their cries is the crime.

Prepared for the Worst

I know the day is coming that you will return.

There is a surprise you must learn.

You couldn't break me in my past.

To hide from me in the present?

This future must be pleasant, where you are is irrelevant.

The evil shadow doesn't matter.

No one will obey what you have to say.

So you travel to a time you think will define you.

To make my life waste and paste your face all over the place.

The problem is I remember each time you interfere.

I don't fear you or even hear you.

This is the day you can't change.

The amazing meeting that will alter everything.

I learned that there is always a door into the fantastic astonishing that shows your future promising.

To be alive where this world can't end.

No trace of lingering worries, for evil scurries.

Darkness can't live here.

Courses are clear, and you're heading into surprising sensation.

There is no loop to bring you back to unnatural wandering.

Rain on My Parade

No kind of weather or unbalanced behaviors can dampen my fun.

I am exploring this world of winning and ignoring the bickering of jinx.

Hand in hand I walk without plan but am secure in this love I want more.

They will fill my sky, ready to strike, but won't find me shaking.

My anger at the attempt only accelerates my ascent.

With her whispers in my ear, there is no fear but wanting.

Wanting to live waking up like this, a happy man unmoving.

I can breathe for the first time.

My time line splinters out of loop, for I won't repeat defeat.

Falling in love clarifies one thing . . . this time I won't feel its sting.

Darkness Can't Find

If my life was the weather, it would never rain ever. These are the times I will look back upon and say how the darkness got lost.

There was no cost or long-lasting effect, for I learned how to turn.

I saw which way the wind blows and made sure I went the other way.

My history isn't always about misery.

There are times that I'm at my best.

Others where I fall below.

Still, I always continue to go.

I must fight on to succeed and fulfill my needs.

To take in all the highlights to magnificent moments that will define me.

I will ride the wave without getting wet.

My speed won't decrease as I race to peace.

The smile says it all as in this moment of time I do shine.

Picture Success

Look and see the meaning of joy as it finally returns to you.

With a wonder if it lasts forever, you will strive to make it better.

Magnify your eye so a tear never comes.

Brace your back for a stabbing.

Protect the happy so you remain smiling.

Watch the way you walk, for you will not stumble.

Build on the love to be a constant.

Those lips caused this.

Let her wash away every sign of decay, for you are regenerating.

Crystal's Pledge

The door won't open for you.

You can't get in.

A key is missing, preventing your trespass.

These days most enjoyable won't be infected by your deplorable.

Your chisel can't facelift his society.

Absent from your variety, he will party.

Good times that shouldn't end, he sleeps sound.

No storm can toss and turn his tranquility.

Bad luck can't win this gamble.

Sadness won't seep in, for sealed are the cracks.

You lost his number and can't track as he got his life back.

The crazed obsessive as your darkness is reflected.

This pocket of pleasure expands without measure.

Leave this man be, or you'll earn the wrath of me.

Severed Limb

You doubted I would ever amount.

No faith that I would freestyle into success.

Without a face to show wrong, you scheme like the day is long.

A knife in the back can't hold me back.

Accept that my life will be neat.

Leave the kitchen if you hate the heat.

The mockery is your support, for you scream abort.

The fake cheer that you care if victory is near.

In the happiness bubble, yes, your trouble, but I dismiss your twist.

We never got along, yet I was the one that was strong.

Emotionless connection to your string, evil you bring.

Stay in your own world, for only there you're not rejected.

The chill of heartless warms not the giver or receiver but chills to banish the bridge of familiar.

Geek Stupid

You had me fooled because I so wanted to believe.

A false prophet perfect in everything.

Claiming to be intelligent, you showed off your wits in arrogance.

Sarcasm came in silent gestures.

All bad things make a mighty entrance, for the church of dollar showcases the scholar.

Darkness not held back reveals the speech of revelations.

To exile the related strutting your worthless.

A misguided attempt and massive mistake to quake one's perception of your reputation.

You hide your stink in oils and cream, but your day will be extreme.

After the end comes on the day of sadness overwhelming, your days will fade from my tolerance.

I return to erase the ego opened to betray me.

Coming Out of the Confusion

As if I was born to ride the storm, I had survived the worst. The ability to link my thoughts to rhyme had returned by the end of nine. My deepest sorrow and hopes for tomorrow would make it to the world at large. The storm was selected for the third objective. Winds that would alter your path destroying your world stranger. With her appearance, there was no danger. Darkness was forgotten, and it couldn't find me. Owning my life for the first time, I sprung to take it all in. She was in my arms, and for hours no one existed in the universe. This was the reward I could afford. I hoped it would never end, but I existed in the present. There was no sense of worry, for my life was live, and the pace was too fast to dwell.

Out of Hole

To my side the strange was creeping to shield me from the horror that dropped me.

A wish granted that I asked for time after time. The high to the low after I finished my climb. I was rising, but my world was still surprising. The one girl to light up my life was someone that searched for me.

Magic swirled toward my resistance, but the positive layered my conscious.

Spirit Victorious

Some things can't be altered or changed. Confidence always remains
although sometimes misplaced.

Meditate to ponder fate to see what could be.

So much more can come from your core if you just believe.

Embrace the blessing to continue on after being laughed upon.

Only you can clear the stage of tragedy.

A new chapter of laughter, for fallen are the deceivers.

You are an achiever, and with a heart pure, you gain more.

Shadows can't form, for this love can't be shaded.

Hatred can't find the glorious.

Feelings are elevated as peace is reached.

The man of nothing gains some weight.

Joy may be late, but love finds its place.

Unlimited Potential

There is no limit or measured limerick.

A line can extend beyond equations probable.

Winds can oppose the reigning evil.

Bad luck will find a different host.

Running out of tears, cracks out a smile.

Out of stock is the puzzle of deformity.

Answers found can unlock spontaneous.

Crazy unexplained fades with an awakening.

High is the swagger of a warrior daring.

Trace a unanimous buildup of fire ashing away troubled fears.

No longer juggle problems meaningless.

Sip the nectar of better.

Tan the pale white to the color of life enjoyable.

A sun won't set after reality's reset.

No more restless hung up on worries.

Sun wakes my relaxed state.

A cool breeze paradises my needs.

Next to me is the happiness possible.

The girl that shocked my heart back to feeling.

Am I still dreaming?

She turns to me with a smile.

Happiness was worth the wait.

My mind is absent of hate.

Is this a sure thing?

I'm lost into passion everlasting as I feel unbeatable.

If my strength has returned, will evil learn to leave me be?

We will see.

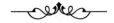

Shadow's Quest

Shadow: Your location I can't detect, but know that I am coming.

I will find a way to break your barrier.

Nothing will keep me from enacting revenge.

My future was a disgrace as you ruled to peace the landscape.

You cost me a loss that I can't accept.

Now you will know regret.

I will change all of time to prevent your climb.

Sorrow will forever trap you in a bind.

Separation leads to depression, and one day you won't recover.

Smother and die to never even know my name.

There will be no one you could even blame.

Just where the hell are you?

Crystal's Vision

Crystal: You can't darken what you can't see.

An anomaly able to run free.

I have been given the power to balance your cost.

This world will continue, for all isn't lost.

The outcome will not be changed.

While you remain, my focus is the same.

He won't see neither you nor me as we are not meant to be.

If you attempt to circumvent, expect my wrath if you alter his past.

I'll cleanse your sin, preventing your win.

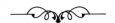

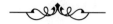

Moment of Achievement

Lift me up away from yesterday. Such pain not knowing time. To suffer the crime of suspension as I lie losing. I don't want to die before I live. Is this the wish that was finally granted? A new world enchanted where I never fall? To rise above it all and not fall from grace? Heaven is today as fun has made me young. No number can slow my pace as I taste the finer things thought missed.

This girl actually cares about how I will fair?

A boost that propels my gears warping the chaos downstream.

I am no longer alone, and my sky is dry.

Whatever the weather, no matter the odds, I'm united in my cause.

All my dreams will come true.

Life begins anew.

Have I Come Home

Is my quest ended as the weary warrior returns rested?

To return to the greatest gift, a beautiful girl different and exciting.

Reality twists, and evil is burned as my life turns to my liking.

A chance of a lifetime with a girl of my dreams, will the darkness team to take it all away?

The butterflies return to my chest as love reaches my crest.

What will be from this melody?

Taste of Nectar

Has heaven heard my prayers, surviving my worst for wears?

A clean slate propels me from hate as darkness can't find me.

I party to celebrate life with new adventures this night.

The loss of confidence mountains my skills.

I'm no longer parched, for I have my fill.

Luck returns, swirling out of control as happiness will chaos the sadness.

I win and I see my future loud and clear.

These books that come from me will fuel destiny.

Many more without question comes a series for motivation.

You will climb and define what you need to see to be happy.

O Lord, my God, thanks for this.

My chance I thought I missed now laid out into eternity.

Heartbroken no more, I have reached my height. Never a lonely night. Believe and you will achieve. Survive and carry on till victory is looked upon. Smile as you enjoy every moment. Laugh for it is about time.

Winds will hit, but never stop this climb. I live, I'm pure, I'll endure. So much of me will be placed across every cloudy sky, searching for sun's surprise. Happiness is realized!

Parade

When I visit this place, my mind goes blank. There is no need for thoughts as spontaneous is excitement. No plans or worries at all as my smile remains. To be with the woman of my dreams is the reward I deserved. My checks are balanced, money remains, and finally I gain. No longer the same, I taste victory. The only thoughts that come are of a future stemmed from this moment in time. Fear is just not here. There is no reason for sadness for my eyes are dry.

I fly in my sky and find no traffic. No noise or turbulence as the weather is perfect. This smile doesn't leave my face. Even if the rain comes, her umbrella stops the drops. Have I finally reached my stop?

Legacy More or Less

Dancing comes naturally like gravity.

This was my father's thing, but it's in my genes.

One day to hold my love in hand and bring her here to dance.

Why do I crave this more?

My father's realm as he graced this place taking trophies home.

I hardly even have the moves, yet this is what I'll choose.

To dance like it's the party of the century.

Closing the book on the sweat and perspiration, for this is my celebration.

Goof Not Looking

As a bumbling fool, you get schooled.

You think you know the way of the world?

Good times never to return?

Learn.

So fast you can't catch up is this enlightenment.

A date you can't believe will lead to this.

Can you handle this twist?

Get ready to be praised for this is your party.

A time so bright that color has temperature.

Scents are noticed, for love is in bloom.

Soon, very soon, this struggle will be worth it.

All it will take is to remove your shades.

You haven't aged and are not obsolete.

One kiss will shift a tide that burned.

To walk without getting wet, your best hasn't come yet.

Your tomorrow is today, have your way.

This isn't the puzzle you could solve.

A life worthwhile?

Don't waste your time trying to dissect, just respect your luck has returned.

Forget about falling down, you're sound.

Not a typical day as none is the same.

On this particular one, your world will change.

You thought you were so smart thinking life held no art.

No more to see, but you made the attempt.

Never to embrace a forgotten pleasure?

As always, never say never.

Get ready to have your theory tested and bested, for you are wrong.

For once it's not good to be right.

This is life.

A gift will be granted, your wish enchanted.

Your time to take in an unexpected place.

Just one meeting will change you forever.

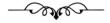

Ageless

A suspension in erosion scaling back to the vibrant.

Youth visits the body not accounting the number.

The heart flows energy revitalizing destiny.

Through joyous experience, the model before the war is assured.

Explore this world without sickness or decay.

Regenerated to enjoy the life denied.

Realize there is so much more to come.

You must be at your best to extend your lifespan through glory blocking worry.

Fear must not wither.

Stress must regress.

Optimism is set on the brightness of possibilities limitless.

Dreams extreme your life to height.

Transform your world into a wish you missed.

Ignore the recording of existence as you won't be labeled exhausted.

Keep Going

Trust that all the fuss must impact the crater of concern.

Wipe away all you learned, for this success is a lesson without a course.

There is no way to explain the motivation.

You can't predict how I tick.

Never to be finished or diminished, I move to never lose.

Stubborn is welcomed, for I don't hear the fear.

I won't stop to accepting doubt.

This isn't what I'm about.

My world is in flux, and I strive without compromise.

The only way is my way to reflect the haters.

God is my only savior.

Unbreakable and Blessed

I'm the stick that refused to snap.

A man that won't be trapped.

I will drive to become realized.

My emotions are known to own.

The seeds I plant will grant you a chance.

Sadness I owned, and now I'm grown to weather a treasure to brightest pleasure.

Some won't let me be, for my success is their tragedy.

Jealousy will strike not right nor understood.

To fight as I should for the darkness won't stop.

I stand against the feeble attempts, for my happiness won't be denied.

Wonderful View Tomorrow

I won't let go of this happiness that grows.

To refuse to be tied to tragedy, I fight the hail.

No amount of pressure can turn me to the dismembered.

My fight will be to show honesty, for the lies will entrap the devious dialect of deception.

There will be redemption and ascension, for your actions can't hold me to dying.

I found my say as I live today changed.

I take in the luck and am pushed to create.

Evil is too late, for I rise tomorrow.

Haters, Beware

My pins won't get knocked down.

My plans will be fulfilled.

Some will not be thrilled, for they can't see me happy.

Everyone has their life to live as mine I build to sublime.

The crime is people bent on my descent.

To pray for me to fail in misery.

If you continue to hate or be my subtraction, watch me take action.

With my dying breath, I will stop your quest.

Let none be allowed to take what little is on my plate.

Worry about your own and your throne.

Focus on your success, not destroying my best.

If an enemy you become, run.

I was the man of nothing but found the one thing to remake me, love.

If you take that away, what exists is the darkness not hindered or contained . . .

Focal Point

Free to run your own saga from disaster, you take it all in.

Hard work pays off as you are living your dream not believed.

A purpose that was created to disintegrate failures achievement.

Out in the open to be noticed and recognized as a winner.

Celebrate life after you survived the final curtain.

There is many a stage that life can be refreshing.

Hope held strong for you carried on to reach that horizon.

Now with love on the rise, you're surprised?

Did you think you didn't deserve this?

The glow in her eyes.

A feeling in your chest.

You're ready for bliss.

Rebound sound

Sprung from the darkest point to the highest star.

Blessed to continue, you can go far.

This gift isn't wasted on being ordinary.

You must climb to be unstoppable.

As daggers are thrown and haters own, be mindful of the escape.

No hex can connect, for by your side is your greatest weapon.

A new love's attention.

This woman so cunning is funneling away evil's say.

Finally your tomorrow is today.

The Underdog Wins

Loosen up, for the free fall is heart-stopping.

Out of control are the days of walking.

Running, not pausing for a grasp of explanation.

Relaxed is the calm to settlement.

A man of nothing, just experiencing.

Look at all you could be if you remain happy.

Sensation without weakness to die.

No effort made to question why.

Laugh it up as you touched the sky.

Adventures vie for the wanderer.

No more alone, you hold her hand.

Hold on to me for this world is exciting.

Back and forth with me, you believe.

I will confidence your questions with good intentions.

If you give me a chance, we will have our dance.

Dark Message Loud and Clear

Shadow: Oh, what trouble will find you.

Your location is set as I connect.

I'm coming to spoil your run.

Silence as trouble catches up to you.

You tried to out run it, but chaos has found you.

Heaven forbids my paradox, but still I surprise.

Tomorrow storms my form to danger your paradise.

Nowhere to escape, racing into wonder, you find me.

The ending I want you to see.

Is your new love enough?

Can passion power your thoughts?

What happens when we cross?

Wonderful Beginning

You won me over with a simple kiss on the lips.

I'm grateful I made the trip that led me to this.

A simple day, not expecting my awakening to love missing.

Lost in the moment, I fear no tomorrow.

I'm not afraid, for a wish come true magnifies you.

A power flows, filling my energy reserves.

The glow that beams peaceful harmony envelops me.

Believe you can achieve what you seek.

Let no evil return to annoy me.

If it tries, I will rise, for sadness must never overcome me.

Peaceful Embrace

When my world was won, I just sat down with my beautiful.

Every day I live this way, for I'm free with this lovely.

No repeat of the worst for wares as I'm rested.

Paradise that feels so right with no sorrow to plague me.

There is no looking back, just ahead.

Expect the Unexpected

Ripples in the pond, a purpose that escapes the rugged.

A mentality that continues to try and reach his peak.

He will never be defeated, for he will never sit still for evil's will.

That smile can't be broken.

His smirk is his token that pays off.

Wild ride with tomorrow in his arms.

He is more aware of what is at stake, for he lived it.

Enjoy this action, for love holds no words.

Just a feeling that everything is fine.

Unwind away from the saddest trip to a survivor's grip on victory.

Rock your way from yesterday.

The dance will come in the brightest sun.

Happiness will never end as a new beginning is screaming to celebration.

Wishes Granted

As the darkness finally found me, I thought I would lose once more.

She looked straight at me and kissed like this was it.

This was far from the end as I would not slip back to chains abstract.

Confidence was still with me and depression was gone.

I smiled, for the greatest weapon I had was faith.

This life mattered, and I would defend it to the bitter end.

There was no way sorrow could return this day.

Light had danced around my space, for it wouldn't give up on me either.

All eyes weren't on me as she was what darkness was looking for.

The moment a shadow would strike, opened be the umbrella.

Evil at this moment wasn't clever.

As a shadow conjured his hex, he learned to his sorrow the word "deflect."

He reached for a say but was blown away by a wind of change.

The fire in their eyes of a new love realized would not be ended as evil intended.

Another day where love had won.

The shadow's attempts have only begun.

Darkness of pain tried in vain.

Now is time for Crystal's reign.

Edwards Brothers Malloy
Thorofare, NJ USA
July 18, 2013